ABOVE: *Glass blowing is thought to have been invented in Syria about 50 BC, though glass itself had been in existence at least two thousand years before then. The blow iron is a hollow tube 4 to 5 feet (1.2 to 1.5 m) long.*
COVER: *The Richardson Glassworks, Wordsley, Stourbridge, c 1830, from an oil painting on board by Emily Hodgetts. The painting shows the interior of a glass cone with the circular furnace containing the pots of molten glass in the centre and the teams of men, or chairs, working around it. The rectangular metal cover suspended above the opening to each pot could be lowered, when melting was taking place, to conserve heat.*

GLASS AND GLASSMAKING

Roger Dodsworth

Shire Publications Ltd

CONTENTS

*Published in 2003 by Shire Publications Ltd,
Cromwell House, Church Street, Princes Risborough,
Buckinghamshire HP27 9AA, UK.
Website: www.shirebooks.co.uk*

*Copyright © 1982 by Roger Dodsworth. First
published 1982; reprinted 1984, 1987, 1993,
1996 and 2003. Shire Album 83. ISBN 0 85263
585 0*

Printed in Great Britain by CIT Printing Services Ltd, Press Buildings, Merlins Bridge,
Haverfordwest, Pembrokeshire SA61 1XF.

ACKNOWLEDGEMENTS
Illustrations are acknowledged as follows: Stuart Crystal, page 1; Sotheby's, pages 2 (both), 3,
10 (left); Christie's, pages 5 (left), 6 (bottom), 25 (right); Trustees of the British Museum, page
5 (right); University of Sheffield, pages 6 (top), 23 (bottom left); British Library, page 7;
Victoria and Albert Museum, page 10 (right); City of Manchester Art Galleries, pages 11
(bottom, left and right), 25 (left); H. J. Haden, page 12 (top); Birmingham Museum and Art
Gallery, page 14 (both); Thomas Webb and Sons, page 18 (bottom); Glass Manufacturers
Federation, page 19 (bottom); Sotheby's Belgravia, page 21 (right); Science Museum, page 22
(top); H. E. Richardson, page 24 (bottom); Bristol Museum and Art Gallery, page 27; Pilkington
Brothers Ltd, page 29. Remaining photographs are by courtesy of Broadfield House Glass
Museum. The cover illustration is reproduced by kind permission of Mr R. Wilkinson.

BELOW LEFT: *Container for ointments or scent called an alabastron: Egyptian, second or first
century BC; height 4 inches (102 mm). Made by the core technique, blue glass with pale blue
threads and yellow rim. Bright variegated colours are typical of Egyptian core-formed glass.*
BELOW RIGHT: *Roman head flask, pale green glass: second or third century AD; height 6¹/₂
inches (165 mm). The head has been formed by blowing molten glass into a patterned mould.*

Diatretum bowl or cage cup, Roman, about AD 300; diameter of rim 7 ¼ inches (184 mm). It was sold at Sotheby's in 1979 for £520,000, then a world record for a single piece of glass and for any antiquity.

INTRODUCTION

Glass is an artificial, non-crystalline material, categorised as a super-cooled liquid rather than a solid. The basic ingredient is silica, usually in the form of a fine sand, to which alkaline fluxes such as soda or potash are added which bring the melting point down to the region of 1300 to 1500 degrees C. At this temperature the glass is fluid like water but before working the temperature is reduced until the glass has the consistency of honey or treacle. Other ingredients in the *batch*, as the mixture of raw materials is called, include lime or lead oxide, according to the type of glass being made, and a quantity of *cullet* (broken glass), which aids fusion and saves on the costs of fuel and raw materials. To colour glass, minute quantities of metallic oxides are added to the batch. About 50 BC it was discovered that molten glass could be blown into a bubble on the end of a long hollow metal pipe, and this forming technique has remained unaltered to the present day. After completion all glass has to be *annealed*, a very gradual uniform cooling process which strengthens the glass by removing the stresses that have built up during manufacture. It is only after annealing that glass is ready to be decorated by techniques such as engraving or cutting. A close natural equivalent to glass is the translucent colourless quartz, rock crystal. Its qualities have been admired and imitated by glassmakers for centuries and today the word *crystal* is widely used to describe the best-quality clear glass.

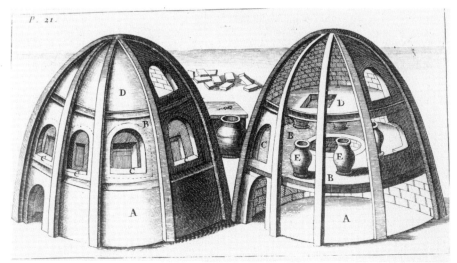

The type of furnace used in Venice in the sixteenth and seventeenth centuries. The bottom section (A) contained the fire, the middle section (B) the pots of molten glass (E), to which there was access via openings in the furnace wall (C). The top of the furnace (D) was used for annealing.

EARLY HISTORY

The Roman author Pliny, writing in the first century AD, tells a delightful story about how glass was invented. Some Phoenician sailors camped one night on a beach, lit a fire and set their cooking pots on blocks of natron (soda), which was the cargo they were carrying. When they awoke the following morning they found that the heat of the fire had fused the sand and natron into glass. But nobody knows for certain how glass originated. The earliest traces have been found in Mesopotamia from the period 3000 to 2000 BC and from there the art probably spread to ancient Egypt. Before the discovery that glass could be blown on the end of a long hollow pipe, various forming techniques were used, such as casting and pressing into moulds, and carving from solid blocks of glass. About 1500 BC the Egyptians began using a technique called *core moulding* to make small vessels for precious ointments and liquids. A core was made from mud and straw or clay in the shape of the object required and was at-

tached to the end of a metal rod. It was then dipped in molten glass and trailed with different colours or it was coated with powdered glass and fired. Once the glass had cooled the rod was withdrawn and the core picked out. This technique continued well after the invention of glassblowing.

Under the Romans glassmaking flourished, spreading from its traditional home in Egypt and Syria to new corners of the empire such as Germany, France and even Britain. By far the most significant event was the invention of glassblowing, which is thought to have occurred in Syria about 50 BC. It led not only to a new style of glass but also to a great increase in production, so that from being a luxury product glass became for the first time a common everyday article — which it was not to be again until the nineteenth century. Cups, bowls, bottles, jars, jugs and vases formed the majority of the output. Roman glass often has a green or brown tint due to impurities in the raw materials but in the second century AD it was discovered that these could be neutralised by the addition of a small amount of manganese oxide. Alongside the ordinary household wares, luxury glass of astonishing virtuosity was produced, such as cameo and diatreta glass and vessels with gold-leaf decoration sandwiched between two glass layers. So skilled were the glassmakers of the Roman Empire that it was fifteen hundred years before the art of cameo was mastered again while arguments about how diatreta glass was made have persisted to the present day. Diatreta vessels are surrounded by a decorative network of glass which is completely free-standing from the body of the glass except where attached by small glass struts. Opinion now is that this network or cage was formed by carving from an especially thick-walled glass.

Glassmaking went into decline in Europe following the break-up of the Roman Empire in the fifth century AD, but the skills survived in the Middle East and during the Islamic period (622-1402) some superb work was produced, culminating in the magnificent enamelled mosque lamps of the fourteenth century. When in turn the power of Islam declined, Venice was ready and waiting to take over. Venice dominated glassmaking for three centuries from 1400 to 1700. Her success was partly due to the strict control which the government exercised over the industry. The construction of furnaces, the months during which they could operate and the fuel to be used were all regulated. In 1292 the authorities ordered that all glasshouses be moved from Venice itself to the nearby island of

BELOW LEFT: *Goblet and cover with an elaborate winged stem. Probably German but in the Venetian style (façon de Venise), seventeenth century; height 14½ inches (368 mm).*
BELOW RIGHT: *Venetian filigree ewer, second half of the sixteenth century; height 11 inches (279 mm). Formed from opaque twist canes of alternating pattern, the style known as vetro a retorti.*

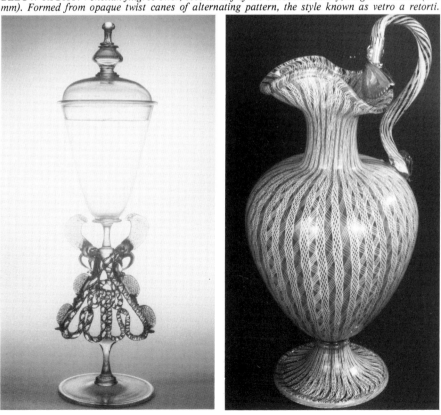

5

Murano because of the fire risk and there the industry remains to this day. The government organised supplies of raw materials from abroad, imports of foreign glass were banned, as were foreign masters from working in Venice, and Venetians who took their glassmaking skills abroad were threatened with dire penalties, even death. A measure of the industry's importance was that in 1940 the guild of glassmakers was placed under the direct authority of Venice's ruling body, the Council of Ten.

Very little Venetian glass survives from before about 1450, when coloured glasses richly enamelled with religious, mythological and heraldic scenes began to appear. Enamel colours were made from metallic oxides and powdered glass as a flux, mixed with a binding medium. After being brushed on they were fired at a low temperature to the point where they began to melt. A little later the Venetians perfected a colourless glass which they called *cristallo*, using quartz pebbles for silica, soda ash from a Spanish marine plant, barilla, and a small amount of manganese as a decolouriser. This was a thin, fragile glass, unsuitable for decoration except enamelling, gilding and light

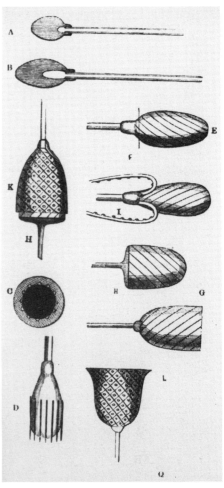

ABOVE: *The technique of filigree glass. Plain or twisted canes, arranged around the sides of a cylindrical mould (C), are picked up on a gather of clear glass blown into the mould (D). The gather is rolled on the marver to embed the canes and then blown out to the final shape. A spiral pattern can be given to the canes by twisting the blow iron while the other end of the bubble is gripped firm (E). The remaining illustrations show how one filigree glass can be inserted inside another to create a mesh effect.*
LEFT: *Goblet by Jacopo Verzelini, dated 1584, decorated with diamond-point engraving, height 6¼ inches (159 mm). It is in Birmingham City Art Gallery.*

A forest glasshouse of the early fifteenth century, probably in Bohemia, showing the small scale of these operations. The annealing chamber on the left is attached to the side of the furnace. In the background wood ash is being refined and carried to the glasshouse in shallow trays.

diamond-point engraving. During the six-teenth and seventeenth centuries Venetian glass became increasingly elaborate. Wineglass stems, previously plain, were manipulated into fantastic shapes and coloured glass was made in imitation of semi-precious stones. The Venetian love of complexity is best illustrated by their filigree glass, in which plain or twisted canes were incorporated in the finished object.

Fortunately for the rest of Europe, Venetian glassmakers did take their skills abroad in spite of the penalties and by the end of the sixteenth century glassworks had been founded in Austria, southern Ger-many, Bohemia, the Netherlands and Belgium, producing glass in the Venetian style *(façon de Venise)*. It was a Venetian. Jacopo Verzelini, who, arriving in London in 1572, led the British glass industry from the middle ages into the modern world.

7

In the sixteenth century window glass was made by two methods: the cylinder or broad glass method, and the crown. Both techniques continued in use well into the nineteenth century. Shown here is broad glass, in which cylinders of glass were blown, slit and flattened out on a table. Unlike crown glass, broad had to be ground and polished after annealing as its surface was dulled through contact with the table top.

GLASSMAKING IN BRITAIN UP TO 1800

Glassmaking was introduced to Britain by the Romans. In the middle ages the industry was concentrated in heavily forested areas, particularly the Weald of Sussex and Surrey, as the glassmakers needed a ready supply of wood to fuel their furnaces. Once the timber in one area had been exhausted they would move on to another site. Their raw materials were also obtained locally, including sand and potash, which was derived from the ashes of beech, oak or bracken. The chief products were window glass and simple vessels, the latter having a characteristic green or brown colour due to traces of iron in the sand.

Glassmaking in the British Isles lagged well behind most of Europe until the second half of the sixteenth century, when, with government encouragement, foreign glassmakers began to settle in England. Window-glass specialists from Normandy and Lorraine in eastern France, some with family traditions of glassmaking stretching back several centuries, established themselves in the south-east, while in 1572 the Venetian Jacopo Verzelini took charge of the Crutched Friars glasshouse in the City of London and produced England's earliest surviving crystal-like glass. Only about ten glasses by Verzelini are still in existence today.

In the seventeenth century two events occurred which radically altered the course of British glassmaking. In 1615 James I, alarmed at the rate at which forests were being consumed, banned wood as a fuel for glass furnaces. This effectively killed the forest glass industry and forced the glassmakers to move to areas where coal was available or could easily be imported, such as Stourbridge in the West Midlands, Newcastle upon Tyne, south-east Scotland,

ABOVE AND BELOW: *Window glass using the crown technique. A large globe of glass with a hole at one end was rotated on the end of a pontil rod in the furnace mouth. A combination of centrifugal force and the heat entering the globe caused the glass suddenly to flash out into a circular disc up to 4 feet (1.2 m) in diameter. After annealing, the disc was cut up into panes. The thicker section or boss left in the centre where the pontil rod had been attached is the origin of the bull's eyes or bullions sometimes seen in old windows and imitated today.*

ABOVE LEFT: *Crizzled glass jug, an experimental piece by George Ravenscroft, about 1674; height 8 inches (203 mm). The metal foot is a replacement.*
ABOVE RIGHT: *Rummer by Ravenscroft in the new lead glass, bearing the raven head seal mark on the stem. By 1677 Ravenscroft had overcome the problem of crizzling and began using this mark so that his glass could be identified.*

London and Bristol.

Then in 1676 came the invention by George Ravenscroft of the famous English glass of lead, which ousted the fragile, expensive Venetian cristallo that had been made in London since Verzelini's day. Ravenscroft, a London merchant, began his researches at the Savoy glasshouse in London in 1673. The following year, sponsored by the Glass Sellers' Company, he moved to a new works at Henley-on-Thames, where he experimented with different materials, including English flints for his silica. Because of an excess of alkali his first glass was subject to a fault known as *crizzling,* in which a network of fine internal cracks developed, destroying its transparency. Ravenscroft's great discovery was that by reducing the proportion of alkali and adding oxide of lead he not only cured the crizzling problem but

created exactly the sort of glass the public was looking for — strong, heavy, brilliant, similar to natural rock crystal. In 1677 Ravenscroft began marking his new glass with a raven head seal to distinguish his pieces from those of his competitors. Ravenscroft's formula continued to be modified after his death in 1683. The lead content gradually increased and sand eventually replaced flints, though the name *flint glass* has stuck. Before the end of the century the new lead glass was being made in the provinces, and much the same formula is still used by the crystal glass industry today, where 'full lead crystal' has by law to include over thirty per cent lead oxide.

These technological advances prepared the way for the enormous success enjoyed by English glass in the eighteenth century. After the supremacy of Venice, it now became the turn of the English style to be

ABOVE: *Selection of mid eighteenth-century English glass. From left to right: mug with moulded decoration; sweetmeat glass; jelly glass; opaque twist and air twist stem wineglasses. Maximum height 6½ inches (165 mm).*
BELOW: *Two Jacobite wineglasses, copper-wheel engraved with a portrait of Bonnie Prince Charlie and a heraldic rose symbolising the Crown of England. Air twist stems, English, c 1760, heights 6½ inches (165 mm) (left), 7½ inches (191 mm) (right). Such glasses were used by supporters of the Jacobite cause.*

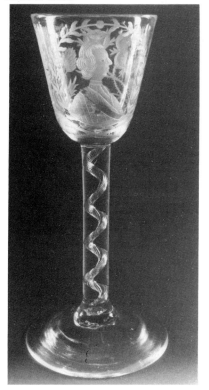

11

ABOVE: *View of Wordsley near Stourbridge about 1900, showing how common glass cones once were in this district. Today just one cone survives in the Stourbridge area, and there are only three others in the rest of Britain, at Catcliffe near Sheffield, Lemington near Newcastle upon Tyne and Alloa, Scotland.*

LEFT: *The Wordsley cone was built about 1795, stands 100 feet (30 m) high and was used as a glasshouse until 1936. It became a listed building in 1966. Restoration of the cone and surrounding buildings began in 1999, and the site is now open to the public as a visitor attraction. Glass cones first appeared in the seventeenth century. The tallest recorded cone was one of 150 feet (46 m) in Belfast.*

admired and imitated by other nations. Eighteenth-century glass is the earliest English glass to survive in any quantity. Commonest are wineglasses with their endless variety of bowl shapes and stem formations. Dessert glasses, salvers, decanters, bottles, jugs, mugs, fruit bowls, punch bowls, candlesticks, even teapots were among the many other shapes made. Unfortunately it is seldom possible to say in which part of the country a piece was produced, let alone in which factory, as the glass is hardly ever marked and style was national rather than regional. Most eighteenth-century glass is clear, though some green, blue and red was made, and there was also a fashion for opaque white glass enamelled in bright colours to compete with the fast growing English porcelain industry. Enamelling on clear glass was practised by William and Mary Beilby of Newcastle upon Tyne in the 1760s but these pieces are rare and highly prized by collectors today.

Engraving and cutting were the two chief decorating techniques used in the eighteenth century. The British engravers rarely matched the skill of their continental counterparts, though they produced some fascinating work such as the Jacobite glasses engraved with symbols and inscriptions relating to the Jacobite cause. Lead crystal lends itself perfectly to cutting as it is a soft glass with a high refractive index and cutting enhances its natural brilliance. Glass cutting was introduced to Britain from Bohemia in the first half of the eighteenth century but its development was hampered by the Excise Act of 1745, which put a tax on glass by weight of materials used. The tax was increased in 1777 and again in the 1780s and was to bedevil the English industry until its repeal in 1845. Ireland, however, was free from a glass tax until 1825 and, once the ban on exporting glass from Ireland had been lifted in 1780, the glass factories at Cork, Dublin, Belfast and Waterford rapidly emerged as the most important centres of cut glass in the British Isles, a position they enjoyed for the next fifty years. Waterford Crystal is indeed a byword for finely cut crystal glass, although the present factory dates only from 1951.

THE BRITISH GLASS FACTORY IN THE EARLY NINETEENTH CENTURY

The most striking feature of glass factories in Britain at this period was the remarkable conical brick structure known as the glasshouse *cone*. Not only did the cone act as a giant chimney for the furnace, creating a sufficiently strong updraught to enable an adequate temperature to be maintained, but it was actually inside the cone that the glassmakers worked, in the area between the circular furnace in the centre and the surrounding cone wall. The upper part of the furnace consisted of a low shallow-domed chamber containing the clay pots in which the glass was melted, arranged in a circle. In the furnace wall above each pot there was an opening through which the glassmakers inserted their irons to gather the molten glass. Below the pots in the centre was the fire on an iron grate, to which air was conducted via an elaborate tunnel system running underneath the floor of the cone. At the base of the furnace was a stokehole through which a man known as the *teaser* fed the coals on to the fire.

The clay pots were a vital link in the glassmaking chain. The special fireclay from which they were made was found chiefly around Stourbridge in the West Midlands, which was one reason why the glass industry became established there. The clay had to be carefully prepared to ensure that it was free from impurities and air bubbles. New clay was seldom used on its own but was mixed with a small proportion of clay from old pots that had been ground down. The pots were built up entirely by hand. When completed they were taken to a special drying room, where they stayed from three to six

ABOVE: *An early nineteenth-century engraving of the Aston Flint Glass Works, Birmingham. Glass factories were frequently sited on canals so that raw materials, fuel and the finished products could easily be transported.*

BELOW: *Inside the cone at the Aston Flint Glass Works, showing the circular furnace in the centre with the chairs working around it. These furnaces normally held between eight and twelve pots. The pot arch can be seen in the background on the right and the annealing tunnel on the left. Notice the young boys working in the foreground.*

Humorous print, after a drawing by Thomas Rowlandson, showing the interior of an English eighteenth-century bottle works. From 'The Tour of Dr Syntax in Search of the Picturesque' first published in 1812.

months. Before being used, the pot was placed in a kiln called the *pot arch*, where it was gradually fired up to the temperature it would meet in the furnace. A pot lasted on average about three months. Replacing a worn-out pot, or *pot setting* as it was called, was one of the most dramatic operations in glassmaking. First the furnace wall adjacent to the defunct pot was dismantled and in the face of intense heat a team of men levered the old pot out. This was particularly difficult if it had cracked and become fused to the floor of the furnace or *siege* with molten glass. Then the new pot was rushed red-hot straight from the pot arch to the furnace on the end of a long trolley and was manoeuvred into position. Finally the furnace was rapidly built up again to prevent too much heat escaping.

The traditional day for pot filling was Friday. First the raw materials were weighed, mixed and *fritted* (partly fused) in an oven called the *calcar* to liberate any gases and burn off impurities. Cullet was then added and the batch was shovelled into the pots, allowing time for one load to melt down before the next was tipped in. Over the weekend the furnace was tended by the teaser, who periodically took samples of the glass. By

Monday morning the melting process was complete and the glass was fit to work.

The glassmakers worked around the furnace in teams called *chairs*. Four chairs normally operated at one time, each making different articles. There were usually four men to a chair, in order of seniority the *gaffer* or *workman*, the *servitor*, the *footmaker* and the *taker-in*. In the manufacture of a wineglass the blowing of the bowl was done by the servitor. He then handed over to the gaffer, who, seated in the glassmaker's chair, shaped the stem and foot from small lumps of molten glass brought to him by the footmaker. The chair had two long, slightly sloping arms along which the gaffer would continually roll his blow iron to prevent the molten glass sagging and going out of shape. Once the foot had been formed, a solid rod called the *pontil* was stuck to its centre. This enabled the gaffer to detach the blow iron and finish shaping the bowl, using a selection of hand tools. Occasionally the glass was taken to the main furnace or an auxiliary furnace called the *glory hole* and reheated to keep it soft and workable. When finished, it was taken straight to the annealing chamber by the taker-in.

Annealing is the gradual uniform cooling

ABOVE: *The Stuart Crystal pot works at Lye near Stourbridge. The completed melting pots in the background stand just over 3 feet high (0.9 m). They have covered tops to prevent the lead crystal glass being contaminated by fumes in the furnace.*
BELOW: *Removing an old pot from the furnace. This eighteenth-century French illustration shows the open type of pot commonly used in Europe.*

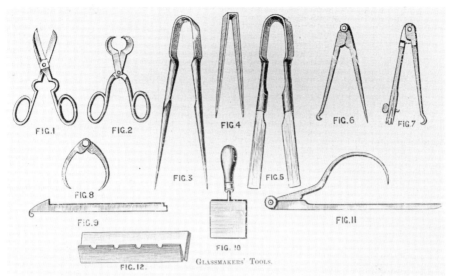

FIG.1   FIG.2   FIG.3   FIG.4   FIG.5   FIG.6   FIG.7   FIG.8   FIG.9   FIG.10   FIG.11   FIG.12.

GLASSMAKERS' TOOLS.

The principal glassmaking tools (excluding the blow iron and pontil rod). Steel shears for cutting hot glass (fig. 1). Parrot-nose shears for cutting rods of glass (fig. 2). The pucellas (fig. 3), the main shaping tool; the prongs have a certain amount of spring allowing a wide variety of operations. Pincers (fig. 4) for seizing pieces of hot glass. The battledore (fig. 10) for flattening glass. The footboard (fig. 12), which sandwiches the molten glass in forming the feet of wineglasses.

process that all glass has to undergo. If allowed to cool naturally, different parts will cool at different rates, setting up stresses which may cause the glass to crack or shatter. In the nineteenth century the annealing chamber consisted of a long tunnel through which the glass was slowly drawn. The temperature within the tunnel gradually decreased from just under melting temperature at the receiving end to ordinary room temperature at the other. Annealing took anything from six to sixty hours, depending on the weight of the glass.

After annealing the glass was ready to be engraved and cut. These operations either took place in a separate part of the factory or were carried out by outside decorators. For engraving, small copper wheels mounted on a lathe operated by a foot treadle were used. The glass was held against the underside of the wheel, the edge of which was smeared with a fine abrasive such as emery powder mixed with oil. Copper-wheel engraving gives a characteristic matt finish, which contrasts

with the rest of the surface.

Rotating wheels were also used for glass cutting. At first they were driven by hand or by foot treadle, but about 1800 steam-powered lathes began to be used, resulting in a deeper, more elaborate style of cutting. The first operation was to mark an outline of the pattern on the glass usually with a mixture of red lead and turpentine. The cuts were then roughed in, using an iron wheel fed with wet sand from a hopper suspended above it, after which they were smoothed with stone wheels and water. At this stage the cuts still had a dull matt appearance. To give the familiar cut-glass sparkle, they were polished with wooden, brush or felt-lined wheels fed with very fine abrasives such as pumice, rottenstone and putty powder, a preparation of tin and lead. This process was both laborious and harmful to health and was replaced in the 1920s by acid polishing, in which the glass is dipped for a few seconds into a bath of hydrofluoric and sulphuric acids.

17

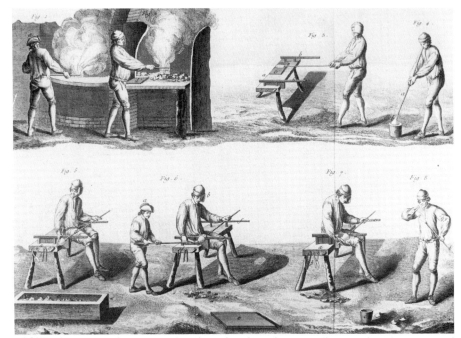

ABOVE: *Stages in making a wineglass (French eighteenth-century illustration): 1, 2, stirring and gathering the molten glass from the furnace; 3, rolling the glass on the marver to get it even; 4, blowing into a mould to shape the glass; 5, preparing the end of the bubble for the stem; 6, attaching molten glass for the stem; 7, shaping the stem; 8, preparing more molten glass for the foot.*

Copper-wheel engraving, in which the glass is held against the underside of the revolving wheel. The pad resting on the top of the wheel keeps in place the abrasive, which the engraver continually has to dab on to the edge of the wheel. Copper wheels range from 4 or 5 inches (100-125 mm) in diameter down to the size of a pinhead.

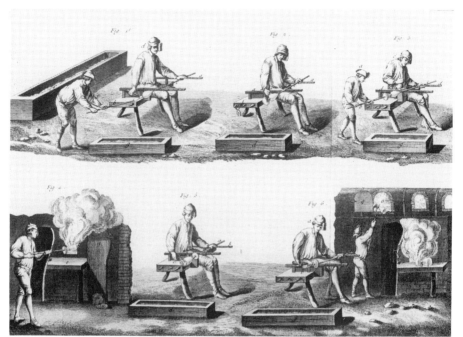

ABOVE: *Stages in making a wineglass: 1, attaching molten glass for the foot; 2, opening out the foot; 3, fixing a pontil rod to the foot so that the blow iron can be detached; 4, reheating in the furnace mouth to keep the glass soft and workable; 5, shearing surplus glass from the rim of the bowl; 6, opening out the bowl with the pucellas. The pontil is then detached, leaving the rough pontil mark in the centre of the foot, and the finished glass is placed in the annealing oven.*
BELOW: *Glass cutting. The cuts have been roughed in and are now being smoothed on a stone or artificial stone wheel.*

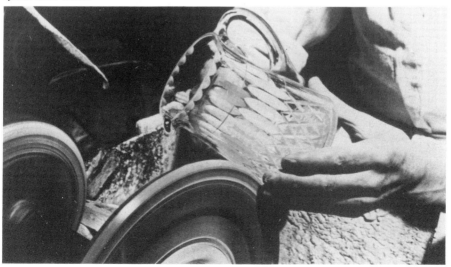

The Crystal Palace was built in Hyde Park in 1851 to house the Great Exhibition. The glazing contract was awarded to Chance Brothers of Smethwick. Using the traditional blown cylinder method they supplied a total of 299,655 panes of glass to a standard size of 49 by 10 inches (1,245 by 254 mm).

THE VICTORIAN AGE

The nineteenth century was an age of progress and innovation in glassmaking in Europe, and for the first time America began to play a significant role in glass history.

Various improvements were made in the manufacture of flat glass throughout the century. One result was an increasing use of glass in architecture, the supreme example being the Crystal Palace, built in 1851 to house the Great Exhibition. A process which was now widely adopted in Britain, though it had been used in France since the seventeenth century, was casting. Molten glass was poured on to a metal plate and then flattened with a roller. After annealing the glass had to be ground and polished to remove the dull finish caused by contact with the metal plate. Faced with this new challenge, the cylinder glassmakers devised a way of producing larger cylinders than ever before, up to 6 feet (1.8 m) long, by

swinging and elongating the bubbles of glass in deep trenches. The greatest triumph for cylinder glass came when it was chosen for the glazing of the Crystal Palace in preference to cast plate. However, about 1900 a mechanical method of producing cylinders was invented in America and this signalled the end of the old blowing technique. A circular disc or *bait* was dipped into a pot of molten glass. As it was slowly raised out it drew the glass upwards in a cylindrical form while compressed air was simultaneously blown in. A little later sheet glass was made on the same principle, drawing vertically from a tank of glass using a bait. Casting, too, was improved, but it was not until the 1920s that the continuous process was invented in which the molten glass passed in a continuous stream from the furnace between rollers and then straight into the annealing chamber or *lehr*.

ABOVE LEFT: *Goblet, acid-etched using a template, Stourbridge, about 1870, height 7 ¹/₂ inches (191 mm)*
ABOVE RIGHT: *John Northwood's copy of the Roman Portland Vase, completed in 1876; height 10 inches (254 mm). It is of blue glass cased with white. These two colours had to have the same rates of expansion and contraction to prevent the glass cracking during annealing. It took several attempts before a successful blank was produced.*

Growth in the use and range of colour is one of the most distinctive features of the tableware and decorative glass of the Victorian period. The pioneering research into the colouring of glass was done in Bohemia and France in the 1820s and 1830s. In England experiment was hampered by the regulations of the Excise Act, but this was repealed in 1845 and by the time of the 1851 Great Exhibition a striking range of colours, including oriental blue, rose, cornelian and pearl opal, were being shown by several of the Birmingham and Stourbridge factories. A very popular colour later in the century was ruby, or cranberry as it is called in the USA. The best ruby was derived from gold though not, as popular tradition has it, from the gold sovereigns that factory managers would fling into the pots of molten glass. Not content with single colours, the American and English factories invented types of glass that would shade from one colour to another, to which they gave exotic names such as Burmese, Peach Bloom

and Amberina. This shading effect was produced by reheating a particular section of the glass at the furnace mouth.

The range of decorative techniques is the other main feature of nineteenth-century glass. Eighteenth-century glass had been dominated by cutting and engraving but in the Victorian period they were just two of many techniques used. A typically Victorian process was *cased glass*, in which the vessel was formed from two or more layers of differently coloured glass. After careful annealing the outer layer was cut or engraved away in places to reveal a contrasting colour underneath. An important new decorating technique which came to rival engraving towards the end of the nineteenth century was *acid etching*. A glass was coated with an acid-resistant wax through which the design was drawn with a pointed tool either freehand or using a template. The glass was then immersed in hydrofluoric acid, which would eat into its surface along the lines of the design where the wax had been removed. The glass could

21

ABOVE: *The technique of cameo. 1, Gather of dark glass cased with white before being blown out. 2, Cameo blank, the design painted on the white outer layer in bituminous acid-resistant varnish. 3, A cameo vase after immersion in hydrofluoric acid. The acid has eaten away all the white outer layer down to the dark under-colour except for the areas protected by the varnish, which stand out in relief. 4, A completed vase after the white glass has been carved with hand tools (5).*
BELOW: *The technique of casing. A gather of crystal glass is being inserted inside a cup of ruby glass. The whole lump of glass is then rolled on the marver to weld the two layers together, after which it is blown out and shaped in the normal way. Photographed at Webb Corbett, Stourbridge, where colour casing was revived in the 1970s.*

then be rewaxed and the outlines filled in with a second etching, using a less concentrated hydrofluoric.

Techniques of the past, such as Venetian filigree glass, were reintroduced, but the most spectacular revival, pioneered by John Northwood of Wordsley near Stourbridge, was the art of cameo glass, which had been lost since the end of the Roman Empire. Interest in the cameo technique had been aroused when the outstanding Roman example, the Portland Vase in the British Museum, was smashed by a lunatic in 1845. Northwood's first major cameo work was a copy of the Portland Vase. It took three years to complete (1874-6) and inspired an important cameo industry in Stourbridge which flourished until the First World War. Northwood had worked in the glass industry all his life but there was a significant development at this time when artists and designers from other fields began to take an interest in glass and explore its artistic possibilities. Emile Gallé in France and the American Louis Com-

22

ABOVE: *The Falcon Glassworks of Apsley Pellatt in London about 1840, showing the type of glasshouse that began to replace the cone in the early nineteenth century. It was a square or rectangular structure housing one or two furnaces connected to a large central chimney which rose up through the roof.*

BELOW LEFT: *An early pressing machine. Molten glass (B) was pressed into a hinged metal mould by a plunger (C) operated by a lever (D). The walls of the mould shaped the surface of the glass, while the plunger formed its inner profile. Only glasses which were as wide or wider at the top than the base could be made by this method.*

BELOW RIGHT: *Pressed glass vase by John Derbyshire, Manchester, 1876; height 5¼ inches (146 mm). Using the press-moulding technique, elaborate surface decoration could be produced literally at a stroke.*

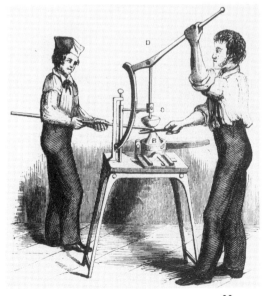

23

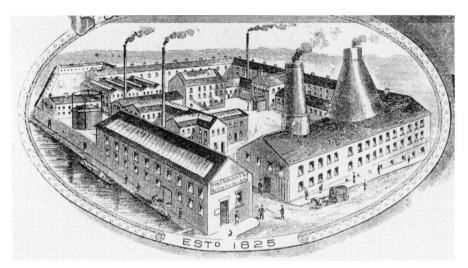

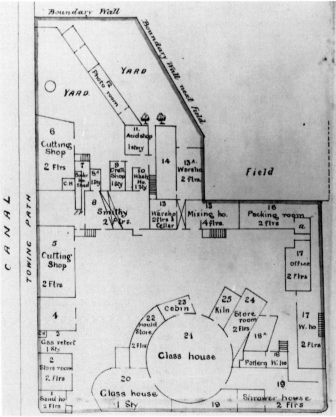

ABOVE LEFT: *Designs for water jugs and goblets by the Manchester firm Molineaux Webb and Company, about 1870. A number of factory pattern books survive from the nineteenth century, which helps in the identification of Victorian glass. One or two firms also began to mark some of their products.*
ABOVE RIGHT: *Lamp made at the Tiffany Studios, New York, about 1910; height 22 inches (559 mm). Louis Comfort Tiffany, along with Emile Gallé, was the leading designer of the art glass movement. He had formerly been a painter. The best public collection of Tiffany glass in Britain is at the Haworth Art Gallery, Accrington.*

fort Tiffany were the two leading figures of the 'art glass' movement, being responsible for some of the most creative, imaginative glass ever made. The freedom which they brought to the handling of the material has influenced glassmakers down to this day.

Mechanisation made surprisingly little impact on traditional methods of production, with the important exception of press moulding, a technique which was invented in America and spread to Britain in the 1830s. Molten glass was pressed into a metal mould with a hand-operated plunger; the mould, which was hinged in two or three parts, was then opened and the finished article removed. It was a quick cheap process that brought glass within reach of even the poorest households. It has been said that two men at a pressing machine could produce four times as much glass as a team of three or four trained glassblowers.

The factories themselves changed considerably during the century. Glass cones ceased being built after about 1830 although existing cones continued in operation. The new type of glasshouse was a much more anonymous structure, in the form of a large shed 50 or 60 feet (15-18 m) square, housing one or two furnaces connected to a giant central chimney which rose through a cast iron roof. The nineteenth-century factory was generally larger than its Georgian predecessor as all the different operations in glassmaking now tended to be concentrated on one site. Besides several glasshouses, the grander works had their own potmaking and mouldmaking departments, cutting, engraving and etching shops, packing warehouse, storerooms and large areas for preparing and mixing the raw materials.

Mr Blades' upper showroom in London; a colour print from Ackermann's 'Repository of Arts', which was published in 1823.

CONDITIONS AND TRADITIONS

The glittering London showrooms which polite society frequented to purchase its glass could not have formed a greater contrast to the factories themselves. Glassmaking was a tough occupation and the glassmakers had characters to match. When the press gang called on the Whitefriars glassworks in London in 1732, the welcome was far from friendly; molten glass was flung at them 'and in hurrying out they ran over their officer, who was almost scalded to death.' The eating, drinking and swearing of glassmakers was legendary, and their physical appearance could be outlandish too. In 1791 a Christian social worker at the Nailsea glassworks near Bristol described the men as 'half-dressed black-looking beings', adding that 'the colliers even are more like human beings than the people of the glasshouses.'

In Britain in the mid nineteenth century glassmakers worked a basic forty-eight or fifty-four hour week. The men were split into two shifts working six hours on and six hours off from early on Monday to Friday midday. Some factories, particularly on the Continent, operated twelve-hour shifts. In the 1860s boys at Nailsea were working a thirteen or fourteen hour day, and sometimes they did twenty-four or even thirty-six hours at a stretch.

Glassmakers were paid by piecework. The factory manager in consultation with the unions decided on the number of each article a chair could be expected to make in a six-hour period or *move*, and rates of pay were fixed for each move, which varied according to the difficulty of the article. If the chair managed to make double the fixed number in its six hours, it was paid double the rate, and so on. Some jobs were more profitable than others and it was up to the manager to ensure that each chair got its fair share of good and bad jobs.

The highest paid worker was the gaffer of the senior chair; he could earn as much as £3 a week, according to one writer in 1849. The wages of a footmaker were about half those of a gaffer, with the servitor receiving an intermediate amount. In 1867 the average wage in the glass industry was given as 28 to 30 shillings, which compared very favourably with other trades. For example, hardware and hosiery workers received an average of 25 shillings, shoemakers, cotton workers, miners and servants 21 to 23 shillings, farmworkers 14 shillings and soldiers a mere 12 shillings. Cabinet makers, printers, iron workers and building trades were on the same level as glassworkers, while only men such as jewellers and instrument makers earned more.

In common with other trades, child labour was used extensively in the glass industry in the nineteenth century, and improvements were slow in coming. For example, it was not until the Consolidation Act of 1878 that half-time working was introduced for children between eight and thirteen and a maximum of twelve hours a day for young persons over fourteen. An apprenticeship for a glassmaker or engraver lasted seven years and the conditions of the contract were strict. For example, the apprentice had to undertake not to marry, not to play at cards or dice nor to frequent taverns or playhouses. His wages increased annually. In 1899 an apprentice engraver aged fifteen received 5 shillings a week, rising to 11 shillings by the end of his term. The apprenticeship system was particularly resented by the gaffers, who saw it

as a threat to their own positions, and apprentices in the glasshouse were frequently given a hard time. One well known ploy was the 'foot ale', whereby gaffers extorted money from the apprentices on various pretexts to pay for their drink.

Some glassmaking processes were very injurious to health. The mixers of the raw materials invariably became ill through their constant contact with the red lead powder used in lead crystal glass. Another source of danger was the cutting shop, where inadequate ventilation meant that the putty powder (a mixture of oxides of lead and tin) used in the polishing of cut glass was continually being inhaled, particularly by the boys whose job it was to feed it on to the wheels. The fumes from the hydrofluoric acid used in acid etching were yet another hazard. Compared with all this, life in the glasshouse was positively healthy. The worst job there was pot setting, during which the men occasionally suffered severe falls, burns and bruises, and they were unpaid for their efforts. During pot setting the glassmakers of Lorraine were said to have clothed themselves in garments of skins soaked in water to combat the heat. However, not all employers were indifferent to the well-being of their men. Thomas Webb's factory in

A very rare illustration showing the glassmakers from the Phoenix Glass Company, Bristol, in procession at the coronation of William IV in 1831. The men are carrying specimens of their work.

Stourbridge was praised in 1841 for its perfect state of repair, extreme cleanliness and — a very modern notion — for the careful railing off of dangerous machines, while in 1845 Chance Brothers built a school for the children of their employees and later organised night classes for the glasshouse boys.

It was to secure better pay, working conditions and education that the glassmakers formed their own union, the Flint Glass Makers' Society, in 1844. There was a separate union for glasscutters. Those who refused to join were branded as Black Rats. At first the employers were hostile to the union and tried to suppress it by refusing to engage union men. Matters finally came to a head in 1859 with the celebrated lockout, when the employers acted in concert and closed down their factories in order to force the union to lift some of its injurious rules. The dispute lasted twenty-five weeks, caused hardship and bitterness and led to the permanent closure of one or two factories. It eventually ended in a minor victory for the employers, but during the rest of the nineteenth century union power was to increase dramatically.

Of the many traditions in glassmaking, one of the oldest is friggering. A *frigger* is a fanciful, decorative, 'one-off' piece of glass made by a glassmaker or apprentice outside normal working hours or in an idle moment for his own amusement. Friggering made a welcome change from normal production work and enabled the glassmaker to show off his skill and experiment with new ideas and techniques. Typical friggers include birds, animals, tobacco pipes, trumpets, bibles, hats, crowns, swords and walking sticks. Walking sticks were supposed to have the power of attracting diseases, and so they were hung on the walls in houses and each morning were wiped clean. If the walking stick was broken, it was considered a bad omen. Glassmakers' parades, processions and picnics were regular events in the chief glassmaking districts and it was on occasions such as these that friggers and other choice specimens of the glassmaker's art were proudly carried aloft and judged in competitions.

A group of friggers, Stourbridge, late nineteenth century. From left to right: birds of paradise with glass fibre tails, bellows, a rat and a swan.

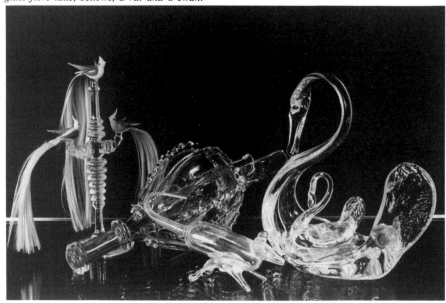

One of Pilkington's float glass lines at St Helens. The continuous ribbon of glass has left the annealing chamber (in the middle distance) and passes into the warehouse on rollers where it is cut automatically into the required lengths.

THE TWENTIETH CENTURY

During the twentieth century there were such spectacular advances in glass technology that glass is now being used in areas that would have been inconceivable in the previous century. One striking example is heat-resistant ovenware, which was introduced in 1915 by the Corning Glass Works in the USA under the famous brand name Pyrex. The borosilicate glass from which it is made has good chemical stability and low thermal expansion and can therefore withstand sudden changes in temperature. In the late 1950s a new material was developed, known as Glass Ceramics, which, like borosilicate glass, is extremely resistant to thermal shock. Its strength comes from the fact that a certain amount of crystallisation is allowed to take place during the cooling of the molten glass, and its applications include cooker hobs and windows for coal and gas fires.

Perhaps the most important technical breakthrough was the introduction by Pilkington Brothers of St Helens in 1959 of the float glass process for the manufacture of flat glass. Before float was invented, most flat glass had to be ground and polished after annealing to remove distortions on the surface caused by the manufacturing process. In the float glass process, a continuous ribbon of molten glass from the furnace floats along the surface of a bath of molten tin in a carefully controlled atmosphere. This not only produces a perfectly flat glass because the molten tin is flat, but it makes the laborious grinding and polishing stage redundant because the glass has become sufficiently hard by the time it leaves the molten tin for its surface not to be marked by the rollers on which it is taken up and conveyed to the annealing chamber. Float glass revolutionised the flat glass industry.

29

Flat glass can be processed in different ways depending on the end use. One of the commonest treatments is toughening, which is done by projecting jets of cold air on to both surfaces of a sheet of glass while it is at a temperature just below softening point. This has the effect of forcing the surfaces into compression while the interior is under tension, thereby strengthening the glass. Toughened glass is about four times as strong as ordinary glass and is used in glazing and for vehicle windscreens. If it breaks, it shatters into a number of blunt, relatively harmless pieces. The other main method of strengthening is lamination, in which a strong flexible layer of plastic is sandwiched between two sheets of glass and bonded together under pressure at 150 degrees C. The advantage laminated glass has over toughened glass is that, if struck a sharp blow, it will only craze, not shatter into pieces, as the glass remains bonded to the internal plastic layer. Bullet-proof glass is an extra thick version of laminated glass. In architectural glass the laminated film can be coloured to give the effect of coloured glass or can have special ultra-violet light-absorbing properties.

The third great area of development has been glass fibre. It is used to reinforce plastics, rubber and other materials in the manufacture of car bodies, boat hulls and protective helmets, and in the form of a glass wool it is familiar as an insulating material for buildings, pipes and boilers. The most exciting recent development, however, has been the introduction of fibre optics for use in lighting and the telecommunications industry. Each optical fibre consists of a core of highly refractive optical glass surrounded by a sheath of glass of lower refractive index. When light strikes one end of the optical fibre it is guided by total reflection at the interface between core and sheath to the other end of the fibre. Fibre optic lighting is used where normal lighting would not be possible, for example in endoscopy, the surgical examination of internal human organs. The most important application, however, is in communications technology such as telephones and television, where electrical signals from the transmitting station are converted into pulses of laser light which travel down the fibre optic and are decoded at the receiving end. Because of their efficiency and cost-effectiveness, fibre optic cables are rapidly replacing traditional copper cables in modern telecommunications.

Container glass and tableware have also been transformed by modern technology. Bottle production, for example, has risen from 2500 bottles per hour in 1907, when automated production was first introduced, to over 30,000 containers per hour today. Even stemware can now be produced wholly automatically, with the most modern machines capable of making up to 50,000 items per day. The real losers in the twentieth century have been the hand-made glass factories of western Europe. Squeezed on one side by competition from glass factories in eastern Europe, the Middle East and now the Far East, where the costs involved in making glass by hand are much lower, and on the other side by the increasing sophistication of automatically produced glass, their products have declined in quality while remaining expensive compared with the competition, and many factories have been forced to close. If those that remain are to stay in business, they may have to go up market and focus on more exclusive products rather than try to compete with the volume producers.

The decline of the hand-made glass industry has been partly compensated for by the remarkable growth of studio glass. The concept of studio glass – glassmakers working on their own or with one or two others in small studios – dates back only to the 1960s, but in the short period since then it has become a worldwide phenomenon. Studio glass takes many different forms, from functional and decorative pieces to sculptural and architectural glass and glass installations, but what all makers have in common is a passion for glass as a material and a general willingness to experiment. As the hand-made industry becomes more cost-conscious and less adventurous, it is the studios that have taken on the role of extending the artistic frontiers of hand-made glass.

PRINCIPAL MUSEUM COLLECTIONS OF GLASS

Ashmolean Museum, Beaumont Street, Oxford OX1 2PH. Telephone: 01865 278000. Website: www.ashmol.ac.ox.uk
Bristol City Museum and Art Gallery, Queen's Road, Clifton, Bristol BS8 1RL. Telephone: 0117 922 3571. Website: www.bristol-city.gov.uk/museums
The British Museum, Great Russell Street, London WC1B 3DG. Telephone: 020 7323 8000. Website: www.thebritishmuseum.ac.uk
Broadfield House Glass Museum, Compton Drive, Kingswinford, West Midlands DY6 9NS. Telephone: 01384 812745. Website: www.glassmuseum.org.uk
Cecil Higgins Art Gallery, Castle Close, Castle Lane, Bedford MK40 3RP. Telephone: 01234 211222. Website: www.cecilhigginsartgallery.co.uk
Fitzwilliam Museum, Trumpington Street, Cambridge CB2 1RB. Telephone: 01223 332900. Website: www.fitzmuseum.cam.ac.uk
Glasgow Museum and Art Gallery, Kelvingrove, Glasgow G3 8AG. Telephone: 0141 287 2699. Website: www.glasgowmuseums.com
Haworth Art Gallery, Haworth Park, Manchester Road, Accrington, Lancashire BB5 2JS. Telephone: 01254 233782. Website: www.hyndburnbc.gov.uk
Laing Art Gallery, New Bridge Street, Newcastle upon Tyne NE1 8AG. Telephone: 0191 232 7734. Website: www.twmuseums.org.uk
Museum of London, London Wall, London EC2Y 5HN. Telephone: 020 7600 3699. Website: www.museumoflondon.org.uk
National Museums of Scotland, Chambers Street, Edinburgh EH1 1JF. Telephone: 0131 225 7534. Website: www.nms.ac.uk
Sunderland Museum and Art Gallery, Mowbray Gardens, Burdon Road, Sunderland SR1 1PP. Telephone: 0191 553 2323. Website: www.twmuseums.org.uk
Victoria and Albert Museum, Cromwell Road, South Kensington, London SW7 2RL. Telephone: 020 7942 2000. Website: www.vam.ac.uk
World of Glass, Chalon Way, St Helens, Merseyside WA10 1BX. Telephone: 08700 114466. Website: www.worldofglass.com

WHERE TO SEE GLASSMAKING

The following factories and studios can be visited by the public. Always ring in advance before visiting, as opening hours vary and some businesses are open only by appointment.

FACTORIES AND CRYSTAL COMPANIES
Caithness Crystal, Paxman Road, Hardwick Industrial Estate, King's Lynn, Norfolk PE30 4NE. Telephone: 01553 765111. Website: www.caithnessglass.co.uk
Caithness Glass, Airport Industrial Estate, Wick, Caithness KW1 5BP. Telephone: 01955 605200. Website: www.caithnessglass.co.uk
Caithness Glass, Inveralmond, Perth PH1 3TZ. Telephone: 01738 492320. Website: www.caithnessglass.co.uk
Cumbria Crystal, The Lakes Glass Centre, Oubas Hill, Ulverston, Cumbria LA12 7LB. Telephone: 01229 584400. Website: www.cumbriacrystal.com
Dartington Crystal, Great Torrington, North Devon EX38 7AN. Telephone: 01805 626226. Website: www.dartington.co.uk
Derwent Crystal, Shawcroft, Ashbourne, Derbyshire DE6 1GH. Telephone: 01335 345219. Website: www.derwentcrystal.co.uk
Edinburgh Crystal, Eastfield Industrial Estate, Penicuik, Midlothian EH26 8HB. Telephone: 01968 675128. Website: www.edinburgh-crystal.co.uk
Georgian Crystal, Silk Mill Lane, Tutbury, Burton upon Trent, Staffordshire DE13 9LE. Telephone: 01283 814534. Website: www.eaststaffsbc.co.uk
Kinver Crystal, Dial Trading Estate, Dial Lane, Stourbridge, West Midlands DY8 4YP. Telephone: 01384 372719.
Royal Brierley Crystal, Tipton Road, Dudley, West Midlands DY1 4SH. Telephone: 0121 530 5600. Website: www.royalbrierley.com
Staffordshire Crystal, Pedmore Road, Brierley Hill, West Midlands DY5 1TJ. Telephone: 01384 77701.
Tudor Crystal, Dial Glassworks, Stewkins, Stourbridge DY8 4YN. Telephone: 01384 393198.
Tutbury Crystal, Burton Street, Tutbury, Burton upon Trent, Staffordshire DE13 9NG. Telephone: 01283 813281. Website: www.tutburycrystal.co.uk

STUDIOS
Aaronson Noon Ltd, Roxby Place, London SW6 1RS. Telephone: 020 7610 3344. Website: www.aanoon.demon.co.uk
Barleylands Glass Studio, Barleylands Farm, Barleylands Road, Billericay, Essex CM11 2UD. Telephone: 01268 290229 or 532253. Website: www.barleylandsfarm.co.uk
Bath Aqua Glass, 1/2 Orange Grove, Bath BA1 5LW. Telephone: 01225 463436. Website: www.realshopping.com
Bristol Blue Glass, Unit 7, Whitby Road, Brislington, Bristol BS4 3QF. Telephone: 0117 972 0818. Website: www.bristol-glass.co.uk
Tim Casey, Sark Glass, The Old Chapel and Sunday School, Nancledra, near Penzance, Cornwall TR20 8NA. Telephone: 01736 741207.

31

Norman Stuart Clarke, The Glass Gallery, 9 Fore Street, St Erth, Hayle, Cornwall TR27 6HT. Telephone: 01736 756577. Website: www.normanstuartclarkeglass.co.uk
E & M Glass, Sarn Bridge, Tallarn Green, Malpas, Cheshire SY14 7LN. Telephone: 01948 770464.
Eirian Glass Studio, The Craft Centre, Hay-on-Wye, Herefordshire HR3 5DG. Telephone: 01497 821346. Website: www.hay-on-wye.co.uk/craftcentre
Firefly Glass, 17 Sherwood Forest Craft Centre, Edwinstowe, Nottinghamshire NG23 9RN. Telephone: 01623 824003. Website: www.fireflyglass.co.uk
Gillies Jones Glass, Rosedale Abbey, Rosedale, North Yorkshire YO18 8SA. Telephone: 01751 417550. Website: www.gilliesjonesglass.co.uk
Jonathan Harris Studio Glass, Coalport China Museum, Coalport, Ironbridge, Shropshire TF8 7HZ. Telephone: 01952 246381.
Isle of Wight Glass, Old Park, St Lawrence, Isle of Wight PO38 1XR. Telephone: 01983 853526. Website: www.isleofwightstudioglass.co.uk
Jorvik Glass, The Stableyard, Castle Howard, North Yorkshire YO60 7DA. Telephone: 01653 648555. Website: www.jorvikglass.co.uk
Langham Glass, The Long Barn, North Street, Langham, Holt, Norfolk NR25 7DG. Telephone: 01328 830511. Website: www.langhamglass.co.uk
Siddy Langley, The Longhouse Studio, Plymtree, Devon EX15 2JW. Telephone: 01884 277426. Website: www.siddy.com
Lindean Mill Glass, Lindean Mill, Galashiels, Selkirkshire TD1 3PE. Telephone: 01750 20173. www.lindeanmillglass.co.uk
Liquid Glass Centre, Stowford Manor Farm, Wingfield, Trowbridge, Wiltshire BA14 9LH. Telephone: 01225 768888. Website: www.liquidglasscentre.co.uk
LoCo Glass, Studio No 2, Brewery Arts Centre, Brewery Court, Cirencester, Gloucestershire GL7 1SH. Telephone: 01285 651119. Website: www.locoglass.co.uk
London Glassblowing Workshop, 7 The Leather Market, Weston Street, London SE1 3ER. Telephone: 020 7403 2800. Website: www.londonglassblowing.co.uk
Allister Malcolm, The Laundry Block, Himley Hall, Himley, Dudley, West Midlands DY3 4DF. Telephone: 01902 311841.
Rob Marshall, Stanstead Park Garden Centre, Rowland's Castle, Hampshire PO9 2DX. Telephone: 023 9241 3122.
Melting Pot Glassworks, White Hart Fold, Todmorden, Lancashire OL14 7BD. Telephone: 01700 81867.
National Glass Centre, Liberty Way, Sunderland SR6 0GL. Telephone: 0191 515 5555. Website: www.nationalglasscentre.co.uk
Phoenix Hot Glass Studio, Riverside Studios, 1-2 Fowler's Yard, Back Silver Street, Durham DH1 3RA. Telephone: 0191 384 7773. Website: www.phoenixhotglass.com
Red House Glass Cone Studios, High Street, Wordsley, Stourbridge, West Midlands DY8 4AZ. Telephone: 01384 812750. Website: www.redhousecone.co.uk
Ruskin Glass Centre, Wollaston Road, Stourbridge, West Midlands DY8 4HF. Telephone: 01384 399400.
Sanders and Wallace Glassmakers, King Street Workshop, King Street, Pateley Bridge, North Yorkshire HG3 5LE. Telephone: 01423 712570.
Adrian Sankey Glass, Rydal Road, Ambleside, Cumbria LA22 9AN. Telephone: 01539 433039. Website: www.glassmakers.co.uk
Scholarship Studio, Broadfield House Glass Museum, Compton Drive, Kingswinford, West Midlands DY6 9NS. Telephone: 01384 812745. Website: www.glassmuseum.org.uk
Shakespear Glass, Foundry Road, Taunton, Somerset TA1 1JJ. Telephone: 01823 333422.
Teign Valley Glass and House of Marbles, The Old Pottery, Pottery Road, Bovey Tracey, Devon TQ13 9DS. Telephone: 01626 835358. Website: www.teignvalleyglass.com
Top Glass, Austcliffe Farm, Austcliffe Lane, Cookley, Kidderminster, Worcestershire DY10 3UR. Telephone: 01562 852166.
Uredale Glass, Market Place, Masham, North Yorkshire HG4 4EF. Telephone: 01765 689780. Website: www.uredale.co.uk
World of Glass, Chalon Way, St Helens, Merseyside WA10 1BX. Telephone: 08700 114466. Website: www.worldofglass.com

FURTHER READING

Battie, David, and Cottle, Simon. *Sotheby's Concise Encyclopaedia of Glass*. Conran Octopus, 1991.
Charleston, R. J. *English Glass and the Glass Used in England c.400 AD –1940*. George Allen & Unwin, 1984.
Cummings, Keith. *A History of Glassforming*. A & C Black, 2002.
Hajdamach, Charles. *British Glass 1800–1914*. Antique Collectors' Club, 1991.
Klein, Dan. *Glass, A Contemporary Art*, William Collins, 1989.
Klein, Dan, and Ward, Lloyd. *The History of Glass*. Orbis, 1984.
Layton, Peter. *Glass Art*. A & C Black, 1996.
McLaren, Graham. *Studio Glass 1960–2000*. Shire, 2002.
Pfaender, Heinz G. *Schott Guide to Glass*. Van Nostrand Reinhold, 1983.
Polak, Ada. *Glass, Its Makers and Its Public*. Weidenfeld & Nicolson, 1975.